Contents

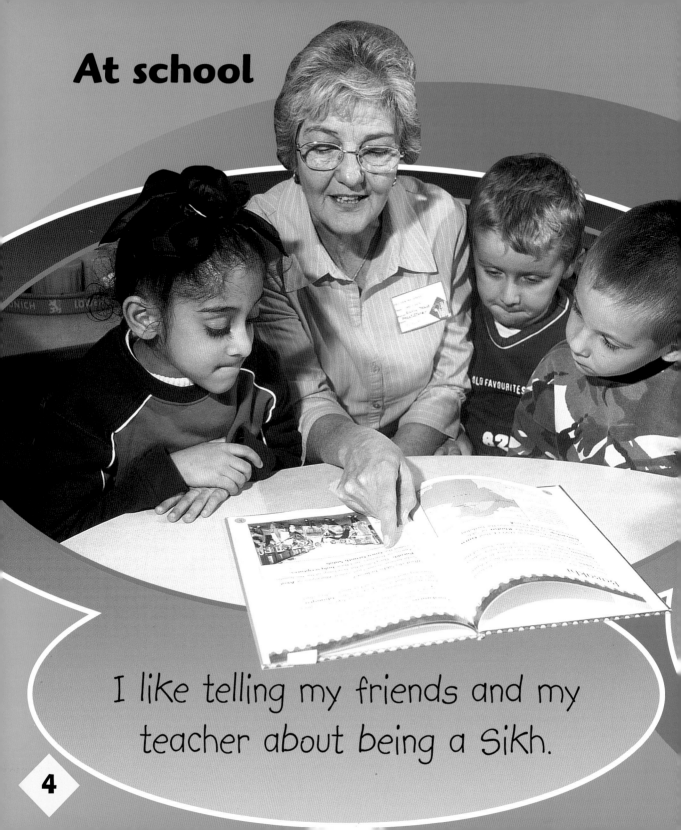

At school

I like telling my friends and my teacher about being a Sikh.

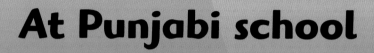

At Punjabi school

I've been practising for the poetry competition. I'm almost ready now.

Mrs Danda is **very good** at playing the harmonium.

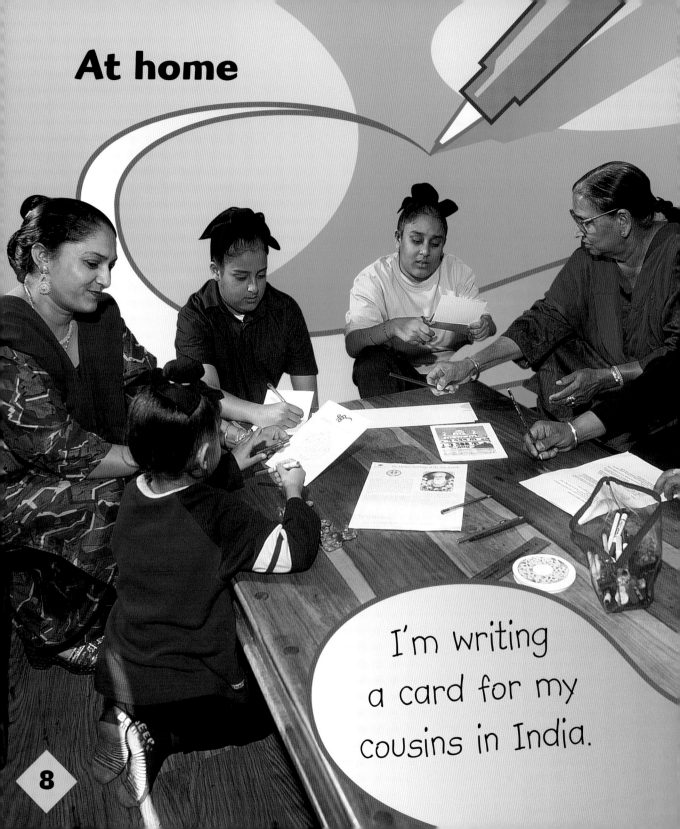

At home

I'm writing a card for my cousins in India.

Don't I look **smart** in my new Baisakhi clothes?

9

Outside the Gurdwara

Baisakhi is a special time at our Gurdwara.

The flagpole is taken down so that we can put up the new flag.

The Baisakhi procession

Here come the Five Beloved.
They lead the procession.

Look! Here come the Gatka dancers.

13

Happy Baisakhi!

Look at that **fantastic** float.

14

I'm really **excited!**

15

Inside the Gurdwara

I'm sitting quietly, listening to the singing.

16

We hear readings from the Guru Granth Sahib.

17

Time to eat

Thank you!

I'm having a helping of karah parshad.

Let's celebrate!

Look at the Bhangra dancers.
They are really good.

The day ends

I love the fair. There are lots of **rides** to go on — and lots to eat!

22

It has been a **wonderful** Baisakhi.

Index

The end

Notes for adults

Most festivals and celebrations share common elements that will be familiar to the young child, such as new clothes, special food, sending and receiving cards and presents, giving to charity, being with family and friends and a busy and exciting build-up time. It is important that the child has an opportunity to compare and contrast their own experiences with those of the children in the book.

The following Early Learning Goals are relevant to this series:

Knowledge and understanding of the world
• Early learning goals for exploration and investigation: Discuss events that occur regularly within the children's experience, for example seasonal patterns, daily routines, celebrations

Personal, social and emotional development
• Early learning goals for a sense of community
• Respond to significant experiences, showing a range of feelings when appropriate
• Have a developing respect for their own cultures and beliefs and those of other people

Baisakhi celebrates the start of the Sikh New Year and is held in mid-April. It lasts for three days and during this time the Guru Granth Sahib, the Sikh Holy Book, is read from beginning to end at the Gurdwara. The flag flying outside the Gurdwara is taken down with much ceremony. The flagpole is cleaned and a new flag raised. There are lively processions in the streets leading to the Gurdwara. After prayers, hymns and readings everyone gathers for a communal meal in the Langar – the dining room in the Gurdwara. There are often fairs and dancing in the evening.